# Biblical Reality

## Walking in the Way of Christ & the Apostles Study Guide Series Part 1, Book 3 A 9-Session Study

Peter Briggs

ISBN-10: 1-947642-02-2
ISBN-13: 978-1-947642-02-7

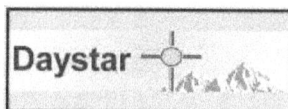

Daystar

Published by:
Daystar Institute / NM, Inc.
P.O. Box 50567
Albuquerque, New Mexico
87181-0567 USA
www.DaystarInstituteNM.us

Distributed in Africa by:
Daystar Institute / Africa
P.O. Box 3989 00200
Nairobi, Kenya
www.DaystarInstituteAfrica.org

# TABLE OF CONTENTS

## LIST OF FIGURES

# Testimonials

"The *Walking in the Way of Christ & the Apostles* (WitW) series by Dr. Peter Briggs is a powerful tool for fulfilling Jesus' universal mandate to make disciples. WitW is theologically sound, conceptually brilliant, and life-changing for those who are trained by it. The impact of WitW is not only personal transformation into the image of Christ, but also a profound influence on families, churches, and the larger culture, whether in America or Africa or anywhere else. Peter Briggs is a theologian of substantial import, but he has not merely plied his theological craft in the halls of academia. With God's leading, he has managed to translate biblical truth and disciple-making principles into something that actually works in the real world! Those who embrace and employ *Walking in the Way* in their own lives will find themselves part of a movement affecting generations to come."

Steven Collins, PhD
Executive Dean, Trinity Southwest University


"*Walking in the Way of Christ & the Apostles* (WitW) is a magnificent literary work in biblical theology that offers the student an education in practical Christianity. The WitW study was first introduced in November 2011; since that time we have been using it to instruct ministry leaders and rural pastors at a low cost, and the transformation of lives is phenomenal. Learners get to understand the message of the Bible and are able to study it effectively. In my own interaction with the material over the past five years, I have come to realize that Jesus Christ is using it to revive His remnant in Kenya and other parts of Africa, teaching us how to think in a biblical way and be successful in all spheres of life. I am convinced that the WitW material holds the key to Africa's revival, and, in Yahweh's hand, it is a mighty tool for returning the continent back to Him."

Michael Mutinda
Team Leader, Daystar Institute / Africa

# Dedication, Acknowledgments & About the Author

## Dedication

The *Walking in the Way of Christ & the Apostles Study Guide Series* is dedicated to Reverend Morris Wanje, whose prayers for God to raise up a means for strengthening and equipping young pastors and church leaders in East Africa caused the Holy Spirit of God to move upon the hearts of godly men and women at Daystar Institute/NM to create this study.

## Acknowledgments

I am especially grateful to Louis Pecasting for creating The Two Ways cover art used throughout the *Walking in the Way of Christ & the Apostles* (WitW) Part 1 materials. I am also grateful for the heroic efforts of our team of contributors, editors, board of directors, and all who have had a part in the development of the WitW study. In particular, I extend my heartfelt gratitude to my wife, Rosemarie, our daughter, Ruthanne Hamrick, and ministry associates John & Marcie Kinzer, Stephen Patterson, and Michael & Antoninah Mutinda, for their valuable input and help with the Study Guide Series; and to Darienne Dumas and Emily Fuller for proof-reading the texts.

## About the Author

Peter Briggs is founder and president of Daystar Institute of Biblical Theology & Leadership Development with offices in Albuquerque, New Mexico and Nairobi, Kenya. In addition to teaching and mentoring, Dr. Briggs has authored the WitW Study Guide Series to challenge students in uncompromising Christian discipleship, practical Christian theology, and building a biblical worldview. The WitW study has had a great impact in both East Africa and the USA, and it is an excellent tool for encouraging and equipping disciples of Jesus to actually live out their faith.

# Introduction

Jesus Christ, in His three-year ministry with His twelve disciples, modeled the method for teaching disciples to walk in His way.

The WitW Study Guide Series is not your usual book-by-book or topical Bible study. Rather, it uses a holistic approach to challenge students to apply biblical principles to their lives and ministries.

This study guide series is designed to equip disciples of Jesus Christ to become thoroughly established in the way of Christ and the apostles according to the Apostle Paul's mandate in Colossians 2:6-7. Our materials emphasize discipleship without compromise, practical Christian theology, and building a biblical worldview.

Bible study teachers and leaders are encouraged to read the WitW Theological Reader Part 1 (TR1) in order to gain a better understanding of the material presented in the WitW Part 1, 6 book, Foundational Principles Study Guide Series. Another excellent resource is TR4, which consists of the List of Resources & Appendices for the entire WitW study. These materials are available through our website or at Amazon.com.

Leaders may use their discretion as to how much material to cover in any given discussion session.

## About Us

WitW is a product of Daystar Institute of Biblical Theology and Leadership Development (DI), which is dedicated to supporting local churches in fulfillment of their mission of making disciples of all nations.     DI offices are located in Albuquerque, New Mexico and Nairobi, Kenya. Please do not hesitate to contact us at www.DaystarInstitute/NM.us if you have any questions or comments, or wish to request training in the use of our materials.

Peter & Rosemarie Briggs

# How to Use this Study Guide

1.  Adequately prepare for your discussion group meeting. Study each session prayerfully, and reflect deeply on the included passages of Scripture as part of your daily devotional time with God.

2.  As a discussion group participant, be prepared to interact with your leader and group members. This includes sharing insights and practical lessons God is teaching you personally.

3.  Read the questions aloud, and stick to the Bible as your sole authority for answers given.

4.  At the end of each discussion session, take time to pray for group member needs; then hold one another accountable for putting the lessons learned into practice.

5.  Upon completion of one book, move on to the next book in the series. In parallel, begin sharing the WitW teaching with family members, work associates, and others in your circle of influence.

6.  We encourage you to avail yourself of TR1 and TR4 to supplement the WitW Part 1 Study Guide Series.

## Overall Learning Objectives for the WitW Study

1.  To learn how to practice uncompromising Christian discipleship.

2.  To become a person who is wholeheartedly devoted to following Jesus Christ.

3.  To learn to walk in the way of God, which is the way of wisdom that leads to life.

4.  To learn about God and His ways through study of His word, both individually and in community.

# Introduction to Book 3

One bright day in the middle of night
    Two dead boys rose to fight.
Back to back they faced each other,
    Drew their swords and shot each other.
A deaf policeman heard the noise,
    And saved the lives of the two dead boys.
If you don't believe this lie is true,
    Ask the blind man; he saw it too.
                   Author Unknown

Absurd, you say. But what is reality? How do we define it? How do we interpret it? Is there a biblical view of reality and, if so, how can we align our thought process to it?

These kinds of questions are important, and we will address them in this study. Our study will also expose us to some terms which will be of interest to those students with a philosophical bent. For the rest, consider this study as essential to our building a conceptual foundation for the rest of the WitW study. The study is designed to provide the framework for understanding at a deep level the principle of viewing reality through a biblical lens – in fact, viewing reality through the eyes of Jesus Christ and interpreting it according to His mind.

Of all our Bible studies, this particular study has proven to be of the most value to our students, especially for the multitude of WitW disciples who are spreading the teaching across Africa.

## Book 3 Goals

1.    To understand that the Bible defines how we must learn to represent reality as it relates to circumstances, events, persons, and things.

2.    To understand that representing reality in a godly way is life critical – that is, it is a life versus death issue. In order to walk in the way of wisdom that leads to life, we must learn to view reality

through the eyes of faith in accordance with the unchanging love, power, and promises of God.

## Notes & Reflections

Formulate a statement of your personal goals and objectives for this study of biblical reality. Also, make note of any additional insights or comments as you begin this study.

# Session 1.
# Two Ways of Representing Reality

## Some Needed Definitions

What is real? The desk chair I am sitting in must be real because I am seated securely in it as I type. Is reality concrete, or is it subject to imagination and preconceived ideas? Are our history books based on reality or the author's perceptions of reality? Is what is real to me also real to you? Is the love of a husband or wife, or close friend real? Is the spiritual domain where God exists and from which He rules more or less real than the material domain in which we live? Just what is reality?

One possible definition of reality states:

> *Reality is the state of things as they actually exist, rather than as they may appear or might be imagined.*

Another states:

> *Reality includes everything that is and has been, whether or not it is observable or comprehensible.*

Both of these definitions assert reality as unchanging fact, whether or not it can be understood.

But how do we humans interpret reality? Someone once said, "After you've heard two eyewitness accounts of an auto accident, you begin to worry about history." We humans invariably bring our personal experiences, intuition, imagination, and cultural biases to bear upon the interpretation of reality as we see it. The result can be many different perceived realities regarding the same incident.

We call how we view persons, events, circumstances, or things **representations**. For example, a person might represent his last vacation as the most relaxing ever, while his spouse might represent it as the worst ever.

Our physical senses (sight, sound, smell, taste, and touch) are the source of input from the material time-space world in which we presently live. We process that input information in our brains through a mental filter that is the product of our culture, education, lived experiences, heritage, media, friends, faith, etc. We call this mental filter our **representational world**. It determines how we view every aspect of the material time-space world in which we live. While each of us has one, it is such a natural and intuitive part of our being that we may not be aware of the profound effect it exerts.

1.      Why do you suppose we use the term "representational world" to describe the mental filter through which each of us views the material time-space world in which we live, move, and have our being?

The reason is this: **it is the world which we actually inhabit**. In other words, the manner in which I relate to and interact with all the persons, events, circumstances, and things in the material time-space world is not according to the true reality of those persons, events, circumstances and things, but rather it is according to the way in which I represent them in my mind.

> *Thus, my representational world is a personal virtual reality that I carry about in my brain that determines absolutely how I relate to and interact with all aspects of the material time-space world in which I live, move, and have my being.*

2.      Based on your studies thus far, what would you say is the relationship between a person's representational world and the sanctification process?

Following is Romans 12:1-2 according to the way in which I have memorized it:

> **Romans 12:1-2.** I plead with you, beloved brethren, in accordance with the aforementioned mercies of God, that each of you present your body unto God as a living, holy, and acceptable sacrifice – a service of worship rendered with the mind. And do not be conformed to this present age by allowing it to press your thinking process into its mold, but rather be transformed by the renewing of your mind, so that you might prove what is the good and acceptable and perfect will of God. [Adapted from Kenneth Wuest's The New Testament: An Expanded Translation]

Our goal as Christ followers is to view the persons, events, circumstances, and things that make up the material time-space world in which we live through the eyes of Jesus Christ and according to His mind. Accordingly, I submit that the principal goal of the sanctification process is the conformance of our representational world to the mind of Christ in accordance with 1 Corinthians 2:16. This, in turn, requires that the way we process information received into our brains be based upon **biblical representations** instead of our own natural intuition and lived experiences apart from God.

> *Only in this way are we able to represent persons, events, circumstances, and things according to the mind of Christ.*

A biblical representation is where the language of Scripture defines the divine perspective on an aspect of reality; either material time-space reality or invisible spiritual reality. Although some biblical representations are bound to a particular historical or cultural context, most are universal and normative – that is, applicable to all peoples, periods, and places.

An example of a biblical representation that has baffled theologians and biblical scholars from the 1<sup>st</sup> century AD to the present is this: **Jesus Christ represented His return as imminent, even to the point that some who had listened to His teaching and witnessed His miracles would live to see His return.** From the teaching of the Apostle Paul, the fact is evident that he was convinced that he would live to experience the glorious return of Christ. And yet Christians have been anxiously awaiting His return for nearly two millennia.

We will now examine three biblical representations expressed by Jesus Christ in His Sermon on the Mount in Matthew's Gospel.

**Read Matthew 5:21-22, 5:27-28 & 6:25-34.**

3.      How did Jesus represent the act of murder in the first passage?

4.      Is this representation bound to the culture of the Greco-Roman world of the 1<sup>st</sup> century AD or is it normative – that is, applicable to all people, period, and places?

5.      How did Jesus represent the act of adultery in the second passage?

6.      Is this representation bound to the culture of the Greco-Roman world of the 1st century AD or is it normative?

7.      With these examples in mind, list three or more normative representations that you glean from the Sermon on the Mount in Matthew 5:1-7:29.

8.    How would you summarize the representational truth expressed in the third passage?

**Read 2 Corinthians 12:1-10.**

9.    In this passage the Apostle Paul shares his thorn in the flesh experience. How does Paul represent bodily afflictions in this passage?

10.   I have recently been diagnosed as having lymphoma – a cancer of the bone marrow. How do Jesus's teaching in the 6th chapter of Matthew and Paul's teaching in the 12th chapter of 2 Corinthians apply to my condition?

> *We will look at a number of other examples later in this study that will enable us to recognize that conforming our representational worlds to Scripture is a life-critical issue – that is, a matter of life or death.*

In our Book 2 study, we learned that the true narrative of Scripture supports and sustains the teaching or doctrinal content of Scripture. In other words, the doctrine is rooted in the true narrative, and it is authoritative and normative by virtue of the truthfulness of the narrative. In fact, on account of the true narrative of Scripture, the whole constellation of biblical representations that we can derive from Scripture form a cohesive and harmonious network or system. This leads to the following assertion:

---

**The Bible is a representational system.**

---

11.  Would the teachings of Mohammed in the Quran or the teachings of Confucius in the Lunyu qualify as representational systems? Why or why not?

12.  Based upon your answers above, why is the status of the Bible as a representational system unique? Explain the rationale supporting your answer.

# Two Kinds of Faith

Later in Session 2, we carefully examine two kinds of faith. However, for you to make sense of the following discussion, I need to briefly introduce these two kinds of faith.

First, we need to recognize that all people have a faculty that can be called **faith**. A person of the flesh (see 1 Corinthians 2:14), whose spirit has not been quickened, has the capacity to place his trust in things with which he has prior experience. For example, such a person is willing to place his trust in his doctor on the basis of prior experience with that doctor. We designate this kind of faith as **worldly faith**.

On the other hand, a person of the spirit (see 1 Corinthians 2:15), whose spirit has been quickened, is able to perceive the invisible things of God and the spiritual realm. We designate this kind of faith as **godly faith**.

## The Workings of a Godly RW Mental Filter

In the previous section, we defined the representational world as a mental filter through which we perceive all aspects of reality. For purposes of our discussion in this section, we will abbreviate representational world as **RW**, and we will examine the workings of, first, a **godly RW mental filter**, and then an **ungodly RW mental filter**. Figure 1 delineates the workings of a godly RW mental filter.

There are three important lines in Figure 1, which are defined as follows:

**Line A**. Working through the agency of godly faith, the Holy Spirit enables the believer to conform his RW mental filter to God's definition of reality as revealed in Scripture. Accordingly, he comes to view persons, events, circumstances, and things through the lens of Scripture – that is, through the eyes of Christ and according to the mind of Christ.

**Line B**. The Holy Spirit enables the believer to impose his godly RW mental filter on the information received from his physical senses, thereby interpreting that information according to the love, power, and promises of God instead of his natural intuition and lived experiences apart from God.

**Line A & Line B**. In combination, these two lines represent the practice of the kind of faith that saves in the believer's personality. We have defined this kind of faith as **godly faith**. As we will discover later in the WitW study, godly faith is actually the faith of Jesus Christ implanted and energized within the human personality by the Holy Spirit.

**Line C**. God responds to the practice of godly faith by unleashing the power of His Spirit to cause circumstances to conform to His definition of reality. In fact, He may actually reorder the cosmos in response to the faith of His saints.

13.   Write down one or more examples from Scripture of God changing the order of the cosmos in response to the prayer of faith.

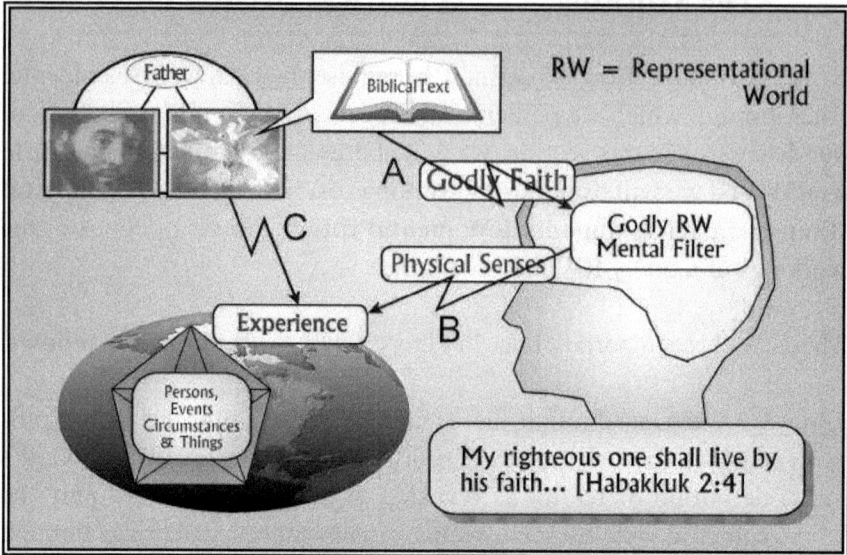

Figure 1. Workings of a Godly RW Mental Filter

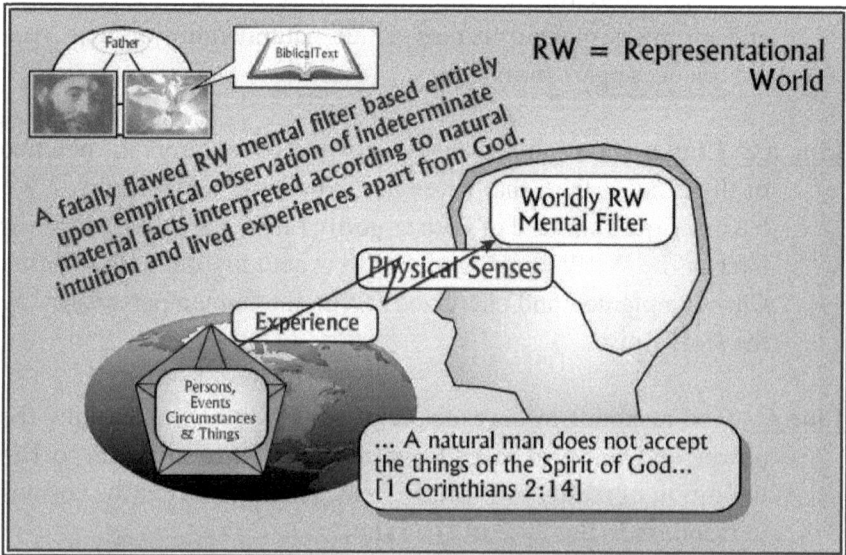

Figure 2. The Workings of a Worldly RW Mental Filter

## The Workings of a Worldly RW Mental Filter

Figure 2 delineates the workings of a worldly RW mental filter, which is based entirely upon natural intuition and lived experiences apart from God.

14.     Having carefully examined both Figure 1 and Figure 2, what critical component is missing from Figure 2 that is present in Figure 1? What is the implication of this difference in the life of an individual?

The worldly faith operating in Figure 2 is not capable of perceiving and laying hold of the invisible things of God.

15.     Based upon what you have seen thus far, compare and contrast the working of a godly RW mental filter with that of a worldly RW mental filter.

16.     Is it possible for a disciple of Jesus Christ to alternate between godly and worldly RW mental filters? How would you describe the spiritual and moral state of such a disciple?

**Read 1 Corinthians 3:1-4 and James 3:13-18.**

17.   Based upon the teaching of 1 Corinthians 3:1-4 and James 3:13-18, how would you describe God's assessment of a disciple of Jesus Christ who is operating with a worldly RW mental filter?

Whenever a disciple chooses to operate with a worldly RW mental filter, he experiences the result of God's withdrawing the power of His Spirit, as represented by Line C in Figure 1.

18.   Compare and contrast the state – including the emotional state – of a disciple who operates with a godly RW mental filter versus one who operates with a worldly RW mental filter. Which state is preferable in your opinion?

# Summary of the Workings of a Godly Versus a Worldly RW Mental Filter

In effect, the person who operates with a worldly RW mental filter is, at least temporarily, **living as if God doesn't exist**. In other words, he is living as a **practical atheist**. In particular, he is, at least temporarily, rejecting God's definition of reality. As a result of God's withdrawing the power of His Spirit, the person actually experiences a reality without God, which is the reality he has chosen for himself. On the other hand, the experience of the person who operates with a godly RW mental filter is in accord with God's definition of reality, which is the reality that he has appropriated by virtue of his godly faith.

# Notes & Reflections

Use the space below to record additional insights and comments resulting from your studies thus far.

# Session 2.
# Two Kinds of Faith

What are the prerequisites to operating with a godly RW mental filter? In this session, we discuss the most important of these prerequisites, which is **faith**.

## Definition of Faith

The primary dictionary definition of faith is as follows: **a strong belief or trust in someone or something.**

Referring to Figures 1 and 2 and the associated discussion in the previous session, we can identify two kinds of faith. There is **godly faith**, which corresponds to the godly RW mental filter of Figure 1, and there is **worldly faith**, which corresponds to the worldly RW mental filter of Figure 2.

All people are capable of exercising worldly faith within the material time-space domain based on lived experiences with certain persons and things. For example, we step onto an airplane because we trust that the airline company has maintained it to be airworthy, and we trust the skill of the pilot and flight crew whom the airline company has assigned to our flight.

1.    Identify some other persons or things that we have faith in or trust within the material domain. What is the prerequisite for such faith or trust? In other words, does it come immediately, or does it require some background of experience with the persons or things in which we have come to trust?

If worldly faith is the ability to have a strong belief or trust in persons and things in the material domain, then godly faith is the ability to have a strong belief or trust in persons and things in the spiritual domain.

> *In particular, godly faith is the ability to have a strong belief or trust in God, His promises, and the things pertaining to God.*

2.   Are worldly and godly faith functionally similar, differing only in regard to the object of that faith?  Explain the rationale for your answer.

3.   Does worldly faith automatically translate into godly faith? Explain the rationale for your answer.

While worldly and godly faith are functionally similar, the fact that a person is able to exercise worldly faith in the material time-space domain does not translate directly and automatically into his ability to exercise godly faith in the spiritual domain.

> *As we will see later in this session, the Apostle Paul repeatedly states in his teachings that the kind of faith that brings justification and the kind of faith by which we live as Christ followers is, in fact, the faith of Jesus Christ energized within us.*

The role of godly faith is pivotal in the development and operation of a godly RW mental filter, for it is the means through which the word of God impacts the mind and transforms long-held thought patterns. Consider the manner in which the following verses represent godly faith:

> **Hebrews 11:1.**  Now faith is the reality of what is hoped for, the proof of what is not seen.

> **Hebrews 11:3.**  By faith we understand that the universe was created by God's command, so that what is seen has been made from things that are not visible.

> **Hebrews 11:6.**   Now without faith it is impossible to please God, for the one who draws near to Him must believe that He exists and rewards those who seek Him.

> **Hebrews 12:2.**  ... Keeping our eyes on Jesus, the **source and perfecter** of our faith, who for the joy that lay before Him endured a cross and despised the shame and has sat down at the right hand of God's throne.  [From the HCSB, emphasis added]

4.     From these verses, what facts do we learn about godly faith?

---

*Godly faith is the means of spiritual perception.  As stated in Hebrews 11:1, by means of godly faith we are enabled to look beyond the things of this material creation to eternal things.  In fact, we are enabled to perceive and understand the invisible things of God.*

# Justification by Grace through Faith

The principal teaching passage on justification by grace through faith is Romans 3:21-26, of which the following is an excerpt:

> **Romans 3:21-22.** But now, apart from the law, God's righteousness has been revealed – attested by the Law and the Prophets – that is, God's righteousness through **the faith of Jesus Christ, into all who believe,** since there is no distinction. [Adapted from the HCSB, emphasis added]

Consider the phrase "through the faith of Jesus Christ into all who believe." Nearly all modern English versions of the Bible translate this phrase "through faith in Jesus Christ for all who believe." However, this rendering is inconsistent with the wording of the Greek New Testament. Interestingly, the Latin Vulgate as well as 19th century English translations are true to the original Greek. Thus, the faith being spoken of by Paul in this pivotal passage on justification by grace through faith is not our faith in Jesus, but His faith energized within us.

5.    What difference does **faith of Jesus** versus **faith in Jesus** make to your understanding of justification by grace through faith?

Consider also the following assertion by the Apostle Paul in the 2nd chapter of Ephesians:

> **Ephesians 2:8-9.** For you are saved by grace through faith, and this is not from yourselves; it is God's gift – not from works, so that no one can boast.

The kind of faith that saves is thus seen to be an **alien faith** that originates outside of our personalities. It is not a work that we can do, but it is a gift from God. We are then responsible for exercising and growing that faith into a rich, strong, fruitful, godly faith; in fact, the kind of faith that will give rise to a godly RW mental filter in accordance with Figure 1.

## The Faith of Jesus Christ

The seven components of the faith of Jesus Christ summarized in Figure 3 are derived from the four Gospels by carefully observing the manner in which Jesus navigated His life and ministry. They are also reflected in His teachings, especially the Sermon on the Mount as recorded in the 5th through 7th chapters of Matthew's Gospel.

Each of the seven components of the faith of Jesus Christ is briefly defined as follows:

**Unshakable love of the Father**. The first component of the faith of Jesus Christ is that the love of the Father for His children (i.e., the elect) is absolute and unshakable. He will never leave us nor forsake us, and He is eager to respond to our cries for help.

**The intimate awareness and concern of the Father**. The second component of the faith of Jesus Christ is that the Father is intimately aware of and concerned about the needs of His children.

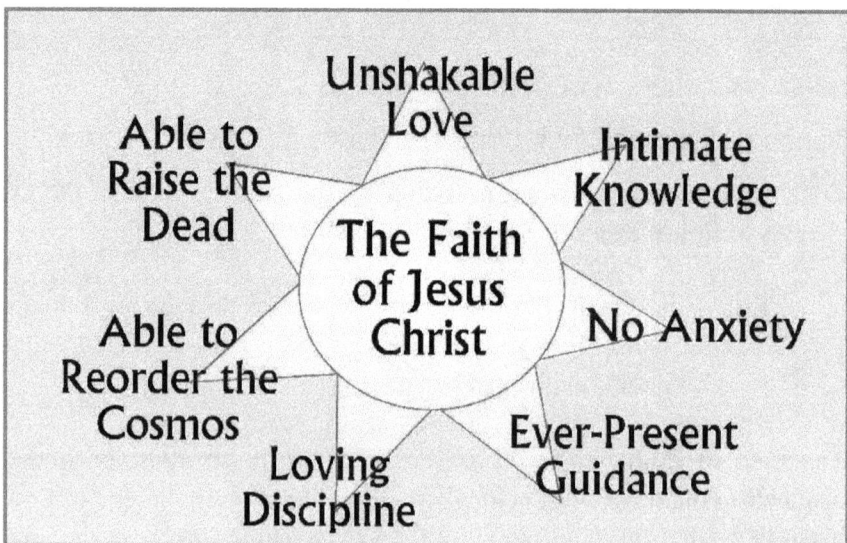

Figure 3. The Seven Components of the Faith of Jesus Christ

Moreover, He is eager to graciously provide for them out from His glorious riches in Christ Jesus if we seek the advancement of His kingdom and His righteousness as matters of first priority.

**Anxiety is forbidden**. The third component of the faith of Jesus Christ is that we must never be anxious. Instead, we must cast all our cares upon the Father, being established in the conviction that He cares for us. In fact, anxiety reveals a failure to practice the faith of Jesus Christ and is sin.

**The Father's loving guidance**. The fourth component of the faith of Jesus Christ is that the Father invariably and unerringly guides us in the pathway of His perfect will if we embrace His will for us individually and His commandments as wholesome, delightful, and precious.

**The Father's loving discipline**. The fifth component of the faith of Jesus Christ is that the Father lovingly disciplines His children. He never allows anything to come against or upon us that is outside of His perfect will, and He causes all events, circumstances, and things to work out for the good of those who love and fear Him.

**The Father's ability to alter the cosmos**. The sixth component of the faith of Jesus Christ is that the Father is eager and infinitely able to change the ordering of the cosmos in response to our prayers of faith, and with Him there is nothing which is impossible.

**The Father's ability to raise the dead**. The seventh component of the faith of Jesus Christ is that the Father is infinitely able to overcome our most powerful adversary, which is evil, sin, and death; even as He raised His Son from the grave, preventing Him from seeing corruption, one day He will raise us who love and fear Him from the grave as well, and cause us to fully become partakers of His divine nature.

6.      Identify a passage of Scripture that represents the practice by Jesus Christ of each of the seven components of His faith as summarized above. The passage can be one of His teachings, the record of an

episode in His life and ministry, or even a promise from the Hebrew Scriptures which He appropriated.

> *A noteworthy example of the faith of Jesus Christ in action is the commissioning of the Seventy in the 10<sup>th</sup> chapter of Luke. In fact, Jesus' instructions to this group of His followers commands them to practice the first four components of His faith, which they had witnessed Him practicing consistently over the course of His life and ministry.*

## The Origin of Godly Faith

Before leaving the subject of faith, a reasonable question to raise is this: if godly faith originates outside our human personalities, what is the process by which it is imparted to us? We believe the answer to this important question is found in the following statement by the Apostle Paul in the 10<sup>th</sup> chapter of Romans:

> **Romans 10:17.** So faith comes from what is heard, and what is heard comes through the message about Christ.

As we read through Luke's narrative in the Book of Acts, time after time we observe the result of the appostles' proclamation of the power-packed message about Christ – that is, the Christian gospel. In some cases, the proclamation was lengthy and eloquent, such as the Apostle Peter's Pentecost message recorded in the 2<sup>nd</sup> chapter of Acts. In other cases, it was brief and seemingly incomplete, such as the message the Apostle Peter delivered to the household of Cornelius as recorded in the 10<sup>th</sup> chapter of Acts.

> *However, without regard to the length or eloquence of the proclamation, it is seen to invaribly energize the kind of faith that saves, resulting in the creation of new spiritual life – that is, people being born again and born from above in accordance with the 3rd chapter of John's Gospel.*

## Summary

The way of viewing reality delineated in Figure 1 results from the imposition of a godly RW mental filter on material facts observed through the physical senses. The godly RW mental filter, in turn, derives from the appropriation of the precious and magnificent promises of God through the medium of godly faith. Godly faith is energized within the human personality by the power-packed message about Christ in accordance with Romans 10:17.

In contrast, the way of viewing reality delineated in Figure 2 results from the imposition of a worldly RW mental filter on material facts observed through the physical senses. The worldly RW mental filter, in turn, derives from natural intuition and lived experiences in the material time-space domain through the medium of worldly faith. The circularity of the logic delineated in Figure 2 means that the worldly RW mental filter is degenerate, and therefore fatally flawed.

## Notes & Reflections

Use the space below to record additional insights and comments resulting from your studies thus far.

# Session 3.
# Two Kinds of Wisdom

In the previous two sessions we have examined two ways of perceiving reality and two kinds of faith. In this session we will examine two kinds of wisdom – that is, two ways of thinking, speaking, and acting.

> **1 Corinthians 2:14-15.** The **natural person** (*psuchikos*) does not accept the things of the Spirit of God, for they are folly to him, and he is not able to understand them because they are spiritually discerned. The **spiritual person** (*pneumatikos*) judges all things, but is himself to be judged by no one. [From the ESV, emphasis added]

1.      How would you summarize the context of the above passage – that is, the 6th through the 16th verses? What is the focus of the Apostle Paul's discourse in this passage?

From the 6th and 7th verses we observe that Paul is comparing and contrasting "a wisdom of this age" versus "God's hidden wisdom". Allow me to refer to the first kind of wisdom as **worldly wisdom**, and the second kind of wisdom as **godly wisdom**. In the 14th verse a single Greek word, *psuchikos*, is translated "natural person." Given that the Greek word for soul is *psuche*, *psuchikos* designates a **person who is soulish** – that is, **whose thinking, speaking, and acting are dominated by the things of the soul**. In the 15th verse, the single Greek word that is translated "spiritual person" is *pneumatikos*. Given that the Greek word for spirit is *pneuma*, *pneumatikos* designates a **person whose thinking, speaking, and acting are dominated by the things of the spirit**. According to Paul, only the spiritual person has access to godly wisdom. In contrast, the soulish person can only access worldly wisdom because he cannot understand godly wisdom. In fact, godly wisdom is foolishness to him, as Paul states in the 14<sup>th</sup> verse.

2.      After having reflected upon the definitions of *psuchikos* and *pneumatikos*, describe in your own words the two personalities identified in 1 Corinthians 2:14-15, including the spiritual characteristics of each.

**Read James 3:13-18.**

3.      We have observed that the Apostle Paul's discourse in 1 Corinthians 2:6-16 is focused upon two kinds of wisdom, which we have designated as godly wisdom versus worldly wisdom. In James 3:13-18, the Apostle James addresses these same two kinds of wisdom, but with different terminology. Based upon the combined teaching in these two passages, what is the source of each kind of wisdom? What are the characteristics of each kind of wisdom?

## Two Ways of Thinking, Speaking, and Acting

The two kinds of wisdom – godly wisdom and worldly wisdom – give rise to two radically different ways of thinking, speaking, and acting.

**Read Galatians 5:16-26 and Colossians 3:1-17.**

4.     How does the Apostle Paul characterize the two ways of thinking, speaking, and acting in the Galatians passage? How does he represent our responsibility with regard to thinking, speaking, and acting in a righteous and godly way in the Colossians passage?

5.     Based upon the teaching of the Apostle Paul in Galatians 5:16-26 and Colossians 3:1-17, what is the **flesh** and why are its impulses incompatible those that come from the Holy Spirit?

In the 5ᵗʰ chapter of Galatians, the Apostle Paul employs the Greek word *sarx* as a technical term that designates the source or fountainhead of sinful impulses in the personality of the disciple of Christ, and this Greek word is commonly translated as "flesh."

**Read Proverbs 4:23-27, Jeremiah 17:9-10, Jeremiah 31:31-34, and Matthew 15:10-20.**

A way to understand Paul's concept of the flesh is to begin with the Hebraic understanding of the **heart**. From the Proverbs 4 passage, the fact is evident that the heart is the fountainhead of our being. Our entire way of thinking, speaking, and acting emanates from the heart. The Jeremiah 17 passage warns us against the deceptive tendencies of the human heart. The Jeremiah 31 passage states that God's people would receive a new heart on which His instruction is written; this would take place under the new covenant, which was enacted through Christ's death, burial, and resurrection. Because elect Gentiles have been grafted into

Israel, as revealed by the olive tree metaphor of Romans 11, the new covenant promise applies to us as well as elect Jews.

With this understanding of the heart, I believe we can accurately define the flesh as follows:

> **The heart before Christian conversion becomes the flesh afterwards.**
>
> **The process of sanctification, by which we are conformed to the image of Jesus Christ, can then be accurately represented as the Holy Spirit reproducing the heart of Jesus Christ inside the skin of His disciple.**

I believe this is the new heart on which the instruction of Yahweh is written as prophesied by Jeremiah (see also Ezekiel 11:19, 18:31, and 36:26).

## Crucifying the Flesh

> **The flesh, according to the Apostle Paul's argument in the 7th chapter of Romans, is unreformable. I cannot tame or domesticate it, regardless of how hard I try. If I struggle against it with all the force of my own will, it will win. The only solution to the problem of the flesh is death by crucifixion and burial – that is, participation in the death and burial of Jesus Christ.**

We will now examine Scripture passages that address the all-important issue of how we go about gaining the victory over the flesh. The first of these is found in the 5th chapter of Galatians.

> **Galatians 5:24.** Now those who belong to Christ Jesus have crucified the flesh with its passions and desires.

6.    What does the term **crucify the flesh** mean to you? How does one go about crucifying the flesh?

According to the Apostle Paul, God's solution to the problem of the flesh is not reformation, but rather death by crucifixion. The principle of dying to self and living unto God is a key representational theme in Paul's epistles, and also one that Jesus taught repeatedly in the gospels.

> *In fact, unless I am willing to take up my cross and follow Jesus, I cannot be His disciple.*

The Roman cross was an instrument of execution. And so each of us must take up the cross by faith as we joyfully embrace our union with Christ in His death and burial with the result that His resurrection life might radiate through our personalities. I believe this is the most important instance of the operation of Line C in Figure 1.

> *As we embrace by faith the reality of our union with Christ in His death, burial, and resurrection, God unleashes the power of His Spirit to actualize that reality in our present experience.*

In fact, this is the way that we come to share in the divine nature in accordance with 2 Peter 1:4.

**Reread Galatians 5:16-26 and Colossians 3:1-17.**

7.    In Galatians 5:16-26 and Colossians 3:1-17 the Apostle Paul characterizes the lifestyle of a person who is walking in the flesh versus a person who is walking in the Spirit. Compare and contrast these two ways of thinking, speaking, and acting.

**Walking in the Flesh**                              **Walking in the Spirit**

8.      What aspects of the flesh in your life need to be conformed to Christ's death and burial?

9.      What does the term **walk in the Spirit** mean to you? How does one go about walking in the Spirit? (**Hint**: Refer to the faith of Jesus Christ discussed in the previous session in connection with Figure 3. In particular, consider the 4$^{th}$ component of the faith of Jesus Christ.)

According to the Apostle Paul in Galatians 5:16-26 and Colossians 3:1-17, walking in the Spirit and walking in the flesh are polar opposite ways of thinking, speaking, and acting. For the disciple of Christ, walking in the flesh is a possible but abnormal state, and one that should be promptly recognized and rejected. Walking in the Spirit is the normal state for the disciple of Christ. It results from the operation of godly faith, which includes the conviction that God is eager to guide us along His way, provided we are absolutely committed to obeying His righteous commands.

**Read Romans 8:1-17.**

In this passage, the Apostle Paul addresses the following questions:

■      Is it possible for a true disciple of Jesus Christ to think, speak, and act in accordance with the flesh?

- Is it possible for a true disciple of Jesus Christ to be pleasing to God while thinking, speaking, and acting in accordance with the flesh?

- What is the ultimate consequence of thinking, speaking, and acting in accordance with the flesh?

10. After having studied the passage, how would you answer these three questions?

11. Based upon your studies thus far, what do you think is the probable cause of a disciple of Jesus Christ falling into sin?

**1 John 1:9.** If we confess our sins, He is faithful and righteous to forgive us our sins and to cleanse us from all unrighteousness.

12. What is the remedy for a disciple's lapse into sin? What does confession involve?

The Greek verb translated as "confess" is *homologeo*, which literally means to say the same thing.

> *In other words, confession is a representational act of the human mind which involves agreeing with God's representation of the sinful thought, word, or deed.*

13.   With this understanding of confession, what is the relationship between confession and repentance?

**2 Corinthians 5:17.** Therefore, if anyone is in Christ, he is a new creation; old things have passed away, and look, new things have come.

14.   How does this verse relate to the two ways of thinking, speaking, and acting?

## Summary

In this and the previous two sessions we have discussed the following two parallel sets of concepts:

| **Walking in the Flesh** | **Walking in the Spirit** |
|---|---|
| Soulish person | Spiritual person |
| Worldly faith | Godly faith |
| Worldly wisdom | Godly wisdom |
| Worldly RW mental filter | Godly RW mental filter |

15.   As a concluding exercise for this session, discuss the connections among the above two parallel sets of concepts. In particular, relate each of the four concepts in the left column to walking in the flesh – that is, thinking, speaking, and acting in accordance with the flesh. And relate each of the four concepts in the right column to

walking in the Spirit. Prepare a flowchart to delineate the logical progression from concept to concept.

Faith is really the starting point for the progression of ideas addressed in this and the previous two sessions and listed above. Consider the soulish person of 1 Corinthians 2:14, who is represented by the Greek word *psuchikos*. Because the source of godly faith is the message about Christ in accordance with Romans 10:17, and because that message is foolishness to the soulish person, he is limited to worldly faith, worldly wisdom, and a worldly RW mental filter. Accordingly, he perceives persons, events, circumstances, and things in accordance with his natural intuition and lived experiences apart from God. Such a person can only walk in the flesh.

On the other hand, consider the person who is spiritual, as represented by the Greek word *pneumatikos* in 1 Corinthians 2:15. He embraces the message about Christ. As a result, godly faith is energized in his personality, he is able to access and practice godly wisdom, and he is able to operate with a godly RW mental filter.

*In other words, he is able to perceive and relate to persons, events, circumstances, and things through the eyes of Christ and according to the mind of Christ. In response to his godly faith, God unleashes the power of His Spirit on his behalf. These are the prerequisites for walking in the Spirit.*

What about the disciple of Jesus Christ who temporarily chooses to walk in the flesh – that is, as if God doesn't exist. Although capable of exercising godly faith, he limits himself to worldly faith. In this mode of operation, he is limited to worldly wisdom and a worldly RW mental filter. In response to his failure to exercise godly faith, God temporarily withdraws the power of His Spirit.

> *However, this doesn't mean that the Holy Spirit leaves the disciple; only that the power of the Spirit is absent.*

Regarding the identity of the flesh, I offered the insight that the heart before Christian conversion becomes the flesh afterwards. While it is certainly true that people who are not disciples of Jesus Christ are capable of virtuous behavior, we can confidently assert that all of us fall short of the virtue of Jesus Christ. In fact, compared with Him, we are wicked and full of iniquity. And so God's solution to the problem of the flesh is not reformation, but rather union with Christ in His death, burial, and resurrection.

## Notes & Reflections

Use the space below to record additional insights and comments resulting from your studies thus far.

# Session 4.
# Example from the Hebrew Scriptures

The Bible is filled with examples of godly and worldly ways of thinking, speaking, and acting. In this session we will explore an important example from the Hebrew Scriptures that is rich with lessons for our lives and ministries. Our discussion in the previous three sessions provides the tools for analyzing this example.

## The Kadesh-Barnea Episode

The principal record of the Kadesh-Barnea episode is contained in the 13th and 14th chapters of Numbers. An abbreviated summary of this episode is presented in Deuteronomy 1:19-46.

**Read Numbers 13-14.**

Beginning with the 9th chapter, the book of Numbers traces the journey of the people of Israel from Mt. Sinai to Kadesh-Barnea, which is located in the Wilderness of Paran at the southern boundary of the land of Canaan. While encamped at this location, they were faced with a crisis of faith that required a choice. Should they enter the promised land from Kadesh-Barnea or not? Moses commissioned twelve men, one from each of the twelve tribes of Israel, to spy out the land. They were to assess the military strength of the inhabitants, the degree of fortification of their cites, and the agricultural fertility of the land. After 40 days, the twelve spies brought back their report to Moses and the people.

The account in the 13th and 14th chapters of Numbers divides the twelve spies into two groups: two of the spies, Caleb and Joshua, form one group; and the remaining ten spies form the other. All twelve men had been exposed to identically the same material facts concerning the land and its inhabitants.

By referring to Figures 1 and 2 and applying the results of our studies in Sessions 1-3, we will now analyze the report of the ten spies versus the one presented by Caleb and Joshua.

1.  What representations did both groups of spies hold in common regarding the following?

    a.  Agricultural fertility of the land (Numbers 13:23-24 & 27).

    b.  Fortification of cities (Numbers 13:28).

    c.  Military strength of the people of the land (Numbers 13:28).

2.  How did Caleb and Joshua represent the fortified cities and the giants?  Through what kind of RW mental filter did they perceive the fortified cities and the giants?

3.  How did the other ten spies represent the fortified cities and the giants?  Through what kind of RW mental filter did they perceive the fortified cities and the giants?

4.  How did the community respond to the two different reports, and what was the result of the community's decision?

5.  What was God's response to the decision of the people?

6.    What lessons can we learn from this episode?

Consider the time line for the Israelite's journey from Egypt to Kadesh-Barnea: after their departure from Egypt, only about three weeks were required for them to reach Mt. Sinai. They remained encamped at Mt. Sinai for 13 months, during which time they received the law and built the Tabernacle. Accordingly, I estimate that they reached Kadesh-Barnea about 18 months after their departure from Egypt. Their failure to enter the promised land through God's front door cost them 38 more years of wilderness wandering.

The Kadesh-Barnea episode is an excellent example of men representing the same situation differently. Both groups of spies agreed that the land was agriculturally rich – in fact, a land flowing with milk and honey. They also both agreed that a number of cities were heavily fortified, and that some of the land's inhabitants were giants.

However, Caleb and Joshua exercised godly faith with respect to these material facts, which means they processed what they had observed through a godly RW mental filter. On the other hand, the ten spies exercised worldly faith with respect to the same material facts, with the result that they processed what they had observed through a worldly RW mental filter. Let's examine the precious and magnificent promises in which Caleb and Joshua trusted, and which the other ten spies failed to trust.

**Read Genesis 15.**

7.    In this important chapter, Yahweh confirms two of the promises that He had initially made to Abraham back in the 12$^{th}$ chapter of Genesis. What are the two promises?

8.    By what means did Yahweh confirm each of these two promises? In particular, by what means did Yahweh secure His promise of the land of Canaan to Abraham and his descendants?

**Read Leviticus 26:3-8.**

9.    What specific promise is set forth in this passage regarding the military strength of the army of Israel versus the strength of their enemies?

In the Genesis 15 passage, Yahweh secured His promise of the land by means of an inviolable blood covenant, and in the Leviticus 26 passage, He promised to exert a one hundredfold force multiplier such that 100 Israelites would be able to defeat an opposing force of 10,000.

10.   In view of these promises, how would you represent the behavior of the ten spies, and then the entire Israelite community, from Yahweh's perspective?

**Read Hebrews 3:7 – 4:13 & 11:30-31.**

11.   What commentary do these two passages provide on the Kadesh-Barnea episode as compared and contrasted with the Conquest episode under the command of Joshua, which occurred some 38 years later? (**Hint**: In your answer, focus especially on Hebrews 3:8 & 4:2; also, apply the results of our studies in the preceding three sessions.)

**Read Joshua 6.**

Beginning with the city of Jericho, the later generation succeeded in conquering the Canaanite city-states throughout the central hill country, then the southern foothills, and finally the northern hill country of the land of Canaan.   Let's designate this generation of Israelites the **Conquest Generation**.  The previous generation, who failed to trust Yahweh, is designated the **Kadesh-Barnea Generation**.

12.   Compare and contrast the Kadesh-Barnea Generation with the Conquest Generation.  What was the key difference between the two generations?  Why did the Conquest Generation succeed in entering the promised land while the Kadesh-Barnea Generation failed to do so?  (**Hint**: In your answer, bring to bear Figures 1 and 2 and the results of your studies in the preceding three sessions.)

> **Hebrews 4:2-3.**  For we also have received the good news just as they did; but the message they heard did not benefit them, since they were not united with those who heard it in faith  (for we who have believed enter the rest), in keeping with what He has said:
>
> > So I swore in My anger,
> > they will not enter My rest.

Notice what this important passage is stating.   There was a gospel preached to Israel through Moses which corresponds to the gospel preached to us.  Both gospels have a **deliverance from** and **deliverance into** component.

13.    What were the deliverance from and deliverance into components in the case of the gospel preached to Israel?  What are the deliverance from and deliverance into components in the case of the gospel preached to us?

Hebrews 4:2 is the key verse in a passage that extends from Hebrews 3:7 to Hebrews 4:13.  In it, the writer of Hebrews asserts that there was a gospel preached to ancient Israel, just as there is a gospel preached to us – namely, the Christian gospel.  Moreover, he asserts that these two gospels are similar or parallel as set forth in the table below:

| Gospel Preached to Israel | Gospel Preached to Us |
|---|---|
| Deliverance from bondage in Egypt. | Deliverance from bondage to evil, sin, and death. |
| Deliverance into rest in the promised land after a period of conflict and conquest. | Deliverance into eternal rest after a period of conflict and conquest in this life. |

14.    Compare and contrast the Kadesh-Barnea Generation with the Conquest Generation in regard to the degree to which they actually experienced the two parts of the gospel preached to Israel.

15.    What important lessons do you derive from the comparisons between the two Israelite generations for application to your own life and ministry?

# Summary

How sad that the Kadesh-Barnea Generation of Israelites, who personally experienced Yahweh's deliverance from bondage in Egypt, and who witnessed the display of His mighty power in the crossing of the Red Sea and at Mt. Sinai, failed to enter the promised land on account of their refusal to trust Yahweh.  Instead, they died off during 38 years of fruitless wandering in the Sinai wilderness.   It was the next generation of Israelites, the Conquest Generation, who placed their trust in the second part of the gospel preached to Israel.  As a result, they took possession of the land under Joshua's leadership.

Likewise, we, as disciples of Jesus Christ, have been delivered from bondage to evil, sin and death.  And, like the Conquest Generation, whose rest in the land was actualized only after a period of conflict and conquest, so our eternal rest is secure, but it will be actualized in our experience only after we have completed our pilgrimage through this life, which is characterized by conflict against the powers of darkness and conquest by the power of God working in and through us.

16.    Compare the faith exercised by the Kadesh-Barnea Generation and the Conquest Generation with the seven components of the faith of Jesus Christ, which we discussed in Session 2.  What critical components were missing in the case of the Kadesh-Barnea Generation?   What was the result of this deficiency in their experience?  What warning should we derive from this result?

By way of conclusion to this session, I would like to quote a passage which I have memorized concerning our eternal hope.

**Hebrews 6:17-20.**   Because God wanted to show His unchangeable purpose even more clearly to the heirs of the promise, He guaranteed it with an oath,  so that through two


unchangeable things, in which it is impossible for God to lie, we who have fled for refuge might have strong encouragement to seize the hope set before us.  We have this hope as an anchor for our lives, safe and secure.  It enters the inner sanctuary behind the curtain.  Jesus has entered there on our behalf as a forerunner, because He has become a high priest forever in the order of Melchizedek.

## Notes & Reflections

Use the space below to record additional insights and commentary resulting from your studies thus far.

# Session 5.
# More Examples from the Hebrew Scriptures

## Messing with God's Metaphors

There is an episode in the life of Moses which teaches an important lesson to us in accordance with 1 Corinthians 10:1-13.

**Read Exodus 17:1-7 and Reread 1 Corinthians 10:1-13.**

The passage in the 17$^{th}$ chapter of Exodus records the first of two episodes in which Yahweh miraculously provided water for His thirsty people. It occurred at a place called Rephidim – a name which means "resting place". Rephidim was located in the south-central part of the Sinai wilderness and not far from the traditional site of Mt. Sinai (Jebel Musa) where the Israelites encamped for a full year. The passage in the 10$^{th}$ chapter of 1 Corinthians contains relevant and important commentary by the Apostle Paul.

1.      What did God instruct Moses to do in order to address the people's thirst issue at Rephidim? Taking note of Paul's commentary, what did Moses' action represent?

**Read Numbers 20:1-12.**

This passage records the second episode in which Yahweh miraculously provided water for His thirsty people, which occurred at a place called Meribah.

2.      What did Yahweh instruct Moses to do in order to provide water for the Israelites at Meribah? Given the representational significance of the first episode, what was the representational

significance of Yahweh's instructions in the second episode? Did Moses obey Yahweh's command?

3.   How did this disobedience mar the representation that Yahweh wanted to present to Israel through these two thirst episodes? What impact did his disobedience have upon Moses' relationship with Yahweh?

God jealously protects and defends the biblical representations He has enacted through His people Israel.

**Reread 1 Corinthians 10:1-13.**

In particular, take note of the 4th verse, which is quoted below:

> **1 Corinthians 10:4.** ... And all drank the same spiritual drink. For they drank from a spiritual rock that followed them, and that rock was Christ.

4.   According to Paul, what did the rock represent in the two thirst episodes?

5.   Why, then, was Yahweh so displeased when Moses struck the rock a second time?

Paul states that the rock that was struck represented Christ. But Christ was struck – that is, crucified – once and once and for all to completely atone for human sin; to strike Him again not only marred the metaphor, it destroyed the picture of the risen Christ interceding for and meeting the needs of His children. Moses allowed his anger to control his actions and thus messed with God's metaphors. Because of his disobedience, God denied him entrance into the promise land.

6.      I believe we would all agree that the cost of Moses' disobedience was great. What application to your own life and ministry do you derive from this experience?

## Review of the Kadesh-Barnea Episode

Kadesh-Barnea represents a watershed episode in the life of Israel. The 12 spies all observed the same material facts concerning the land of Canaan, and they all experienced the same events. But the 10 spies interpreted what they saw and experienced through a worldly RW mental filter, whereas Caleb and Joshua interpreted them through a godly RW mental filter. In like manner, you and I may share similar experiences, but how we interpret and respond to them depends upon our RW mental filter.

The Kadesh-Barnea Generation failed to trust the promises of Yahweh, which engendered **fear**. As a result, that entire generation was condemned to die off while fruitlessly wandering about in the wilderness of Sinai, and they failed to enjoy the promised rest in the land of Canaan. The Conquest Generation chose the way of trust in and reliance upon the promises of Yahweh, which engendered **victorious courage**. The result was that they enjoyed the promised rest in the land of Canaan after a period of conflict and conquest.

**Faithlessness ➧ Fear ➧ Defeat**

**Faithfulness ➧ Courage ➧ Victory**

7.    What impact does this teaching have upon your life and ministry? How do you intend to avoid the way of faithlessness, leading to fear and defeat, and practice the way of faithfulness, leading to courage and victory?

# David and Goliath – Faith versus Fear

We will now turn to another watershed episode in the history of Israel, the David and Goliath episode.

**Read 1 Samuel 17.**

8.    Analyze this passage by applying the tools we discussed in Sessions 1-3 and then applied in Session 4 to the Kadesh-Barnea episode.

The armies of the Philistines and of Israel were facing each other in preparation for battle. However, to humiliate King Saul and the army of Israel, the giant Goliath came forth from the ranks of the Philistines and challenged Saul to select a single man to engage in one-on-one combat. The victor in this contest would determine the outcome of the battle for both nations.

9. Compare and contrast the way in which Saul and his entire army represented Goliath with the way in which David represented Goliath. In particular, what RW mental filter was being employed by Saul versus David?

10. How do these two different ways of representing a single set of material facts relate to Figures 1 and 2?

11. How did Yahweh respond to this situation, and what was the ultimate outcome? Relate this outcome to the lines in Figure 1.

12. What lessons can we derive from this episode?

Like the Kadesh-Barnea episode, the David and Goliath episode provides a clear and dramatic contrast between the result of applying a godly versus a worldly RW mental filter to a given set of material facts. King Saul perceived Goliath through a worldly RW mental filter; that is, on the basis of his past experiences and natural intuition apart from God. As a result, he represented Goliath as an invincible military force on account of his great stature, his seemingly impenetrable defensive armor, and his powerful offensive weaponry. No one in Saul's army, including Saul himself, was capable of facing him in one-on-one combat.

---

**Accordingly, Saul's faithlessness engendered fear.**

---

In stark contrast, David relied completely upon Yahweh and His word. Having seen Yahweh work in his defense against lions and bears while guarding his father's sheep, David perceived Goliath through a godly RW mental filter. Accordingly, he represented the giant as already defeated because he was defying the living God and humiliating the people of God. Thus David, though a young man, willingly stepped forward to fight the giant in the power and might of Yahweh. As he ran to engage the Philistine in combat, he shouted that timeless and normative battle cry of the people of God:

> **1 Samuel 17:46-47.** Then all the world will know that Israel has an Elohim, and this whole assembly will know that it is not by sword or by spear that Yahweh saves, for the battle is Yahweh's. He will hand you over to us. [Adapted from the HCSB]

---

*David's unshakeable trust in Yahweh engendered courage to engage the giant, Goliath; the ultimate result was a glorious victory for Israel and a showcasing of the power of Yahweh.*

---

13. Do you face a "Goliath" in your life or ministry? How can this story help you replace fear with faith? What would that look like in the particular situation you have in mind?

# The Tabernacle in the Wilderness

The Tabernacle in the wilderness is illustrated in Figure 4. Its design, construction, and erection is recorded in Exodus 35:4 – 40:38. The Tabernacle in the wilderness is a rich representation of God's holiness and how we, a sinful people, can approach Him.

> *The Tabernacle's design, furnishings, and associated Levitical worship system offer rich and powerful object lessons in regard to personal holiness and the proper way to worship Yahweh. In addition, the tabernacle and its furnishings provide a poignant representation of the life and ministry of Jesus Christ.*

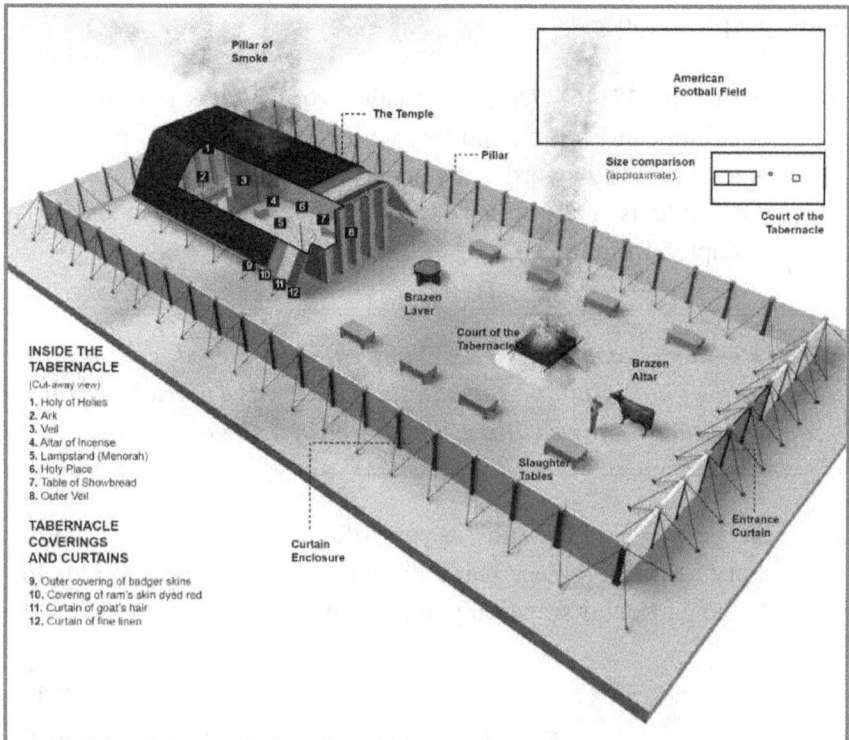

Figure 4. The Tabernacle in the Wilderness – A Rich Biblical Representation

14.    Study Figure 4 and list possible representations of Christ you see in the Tabernacle and its furnishings.

You may have observed such representations as the following:

■     A single entrance to the courtyard – Jesus is the way, the truth, and the life.

■     Brazen alter – Christ is our sin offering.

■     Laver – we receive daily cleansing on the basis of Christ's shed blood.

These are listed as examples for you to reflect upon as you ponder the ways in which the Tabernacle represents holiness, proper worship, and the life and ministry of Jesus Christ.

## Notes & Reflections

Use the space below to record additional insights and comments resulting from your studies thus far.

# Session 6.
# Linking the Hebrew & Christian Scriptures

## The Christian's Relationship with Torah

**Read Matthew 5:17-20.**

This passage is part of Christ's Sermon on the Mount. In it, Jesus makes some important statements concerning the Hebrew Scriptures, and specifically the Torah; that is, the five books of Moses.

1.      Based upon His statements, how does Christ represent the Torah? How, then, should we represent it?

2.      How do Christians in general represent the books of the Hebrew Scriptures?

It is important to recognize that in fulfilling the Torah, Christ was not only authenticating it, but assuring its place in the Christian era as relevant, valuable, and authoritative. In fact, the Torah is a timeless and normative declaration of what righteous living looks like. As we have seen in Sessions 4 and 5, the Torah contains object lessons in holiness and how a sinful man can properly worship an absolutely holy God.

> *Indeed, the Torah is the fountainhead of wisdom.*

**Read Matthew 5:21-23.**

3.     What frightening statement does Jesus make in this passage?

> **Matthew 5:18.** For I assure you: Until heaven and earth pass away, not the smallest letter or one stroke of a letter will pass from the law until all things are accomplished.

4.     How did Jesus fulfill the law?

5.     When will all things be accomplished?

In His life and ministry, Jesus fulfilled all the requirements of the Torah, not just in the sphere of external behavior, but at the level of the thoughts and inclinations of the heart. And through His sacrificial death, He completely rendered to God the Father a suitable apology and satisfaction that we owe to Him on account of our transgressions against the law. According to the words of the 53rd chapter of Isaiah, Yahweh laid upon Him the iniquity of us all, and by His wounds we are healed.

Following is a collection of verses that, together, reflect the view of the Apostle Paul on the relationship between the disciple of Christ and the Torah; each verse should be studied within the context of the paragraph that contains it:

> **Galatians 2:16.** ... We know that a person is not justified by works of the law but through the faith of Jesus Christ, so we also have believed into Christ Jesus, in order to be justified by the faith of Christ and not by works of the law, because by works of the law no one will be justified. [Adapted from the ESV]

**Galatians 3:10.** For all who rely on works of the law are under a curse; for it is written, "Cursed be everyone who does not abide by all things written in the Book of the Law, and do them."

**Galatians 3:24.** So then, the law was our guardian until Christ came, in order that we might be justified by faith.

**Romans 3:20-22.** For by works of the law no human being will be justified in His sight, since through the law comes knowledge of sin. But now the righteousness of God has been manifested apart from the law, although the Law and the Prophets bear witness to it – the righteousness of God through the faith of Jesus Christ into all who believe. [Adapted from the ESV]

**Romans 3:31.** Do we then overthrow the law by this faith? By no means! On the contrary, we uphold the law.

**Romans 7:4.** Likewise, my brothers, you also have died to the law through the body of Christ, so that you may belong to another, to Him who has been raised from the dead, in order that we may bear fruit for God. [Adapted from the ESV]

**Romans 7:12.** So the law is holy, and the commandment is holy and righteous and good.

**Romans 8:3-4.** For God has done what the law, weakened as it was by the flesh, could not do. By sending His own Son in the likeness of sinful flesh and for sin, He condemned sin in the flesh, in order that the righteous requirement of the law might be fulfilled in us, who walk not according to the flesh but according to the Spirit. [Adapted from the ESV]

**Romans 10:4.** For Christ is the end of the law for righteousness to everyone who believes. [ESV]

6.     Based upon this entire collection of passages from the writings of the Apostle Paul, each read within its paragraph context, how would you summarize Paul's teaching in regard to the relationship between the disciple of Christ and the Torah?

7.     How are the righteous requirements of the law fulfilled in us according to Romans 8:3-4?

Even as redeemed and regenerated disciples of Christ, we are powerless to achieve God's standard of righteousness through law-keeping out from the energy of the flesh. In fact, to attempt this results in frustration, discouragement, defeat, and abject despair in accordance with Paul's teaching in the 7th chapter of Romans. While the standard of righteousness expressed in the Torah has not been abrogated, the dynamics for keeping it has been radically changed through Christ's death.

> *We uphold and fulfill the law by the power of the indwelling Holy Spirit and not by the power of the flesh.*

**Read Jeremiah 31:31-33.** Noteworthy excerpts from this passage are quoted below:

> … I will make a new covenant … I will put My teaching within them and write it on their hearts. I will be their God, and they will be My people.

This is the seminal passage that announces the new covenant which Jesus Christ placed into operation through His death. A covenant is a binding agreement between two persons on a relational level. Marriage is an important example of a covenant between a man and a woman – a binding agreement consecrated before God and an assembly of human witnesses.

The Mosaic covenant was enacted between Yahweh and the nation of Israel through the mediation of Moses. The time of this enactment was ca. 1405 BC, and the place was Mt. Sinai. Approximately 800 years later, in the early part of the 6th century BC, Jeremiah announced the new covenant that would replace the Mosaic covenant.

8.      According to Jeremiah 31:31ff, to whom is the new covenant addressed, and how is this covenant different from the old covenant which Yahweh enacted with Israel through Moses in accordance with Exodus 20:1ff?

**Read Romans 11 and Ephesians 2:11-22.**

It is noteworthy that the new covenant announced by Jeremiah was between Yahweh and the "house of Israel and the house of Judah". The "house of Israel" refers to the northern kingdom of Israel that had been conquered by the Assyrians in 722 BC; and "the house of Judah" refers to the southern kingdom of Judah that still existed during the early part of Jeremiah's prophetic ministry but was conquered by the Babylonians and taken into exile beginning ca. 605 BC. In fact, based upon the chronological marker at the beginning of the 32nd chapter of Jeremiah, the new covenant prophecy was announced ca. 587 BC, just before the final destruction of Jerusalem.

---

*In sum, the new covenant was expressly enacted between Yahweh and the people of Israel.*

---

9.  This being the case, how would you explain the inclusion of Gentiles under the terms of the new covenant? What is the relationship between believing Jews and believing Gentiles under the terms of the new covenant?

Jesus Christ has enacted and placed into operation the new covenant through His death. Moreover, God, on the basis of His lavish and unspeakable grace, has decreed that the Gentiles would no longer be strangers and aliens, but would be fellow citizens with the saints and members of God's household. As Paul explains in the 11th chapter of Romans, we are like wild olive branches grafted into a cultivated olive tree, which represents Israel. And so we, who were without God and without hope in this world, have been made partakers of the new covenant promises as those grafted into Israel.

> ***Now Israel's history is indeed our history.***

So we conclude that the Torah remains as the timeless expression of human righteousness. Its normative teachings apply to all peoples, periods, and places. The pattern of behavior it prescribes reflects the nature and character of God, and it flows from a life that is fully devoted to God and His ways.

> ***In other words, it prescribes a pattern of human behavior that brings a smile to God's face.***

10. Based upon all your studies in this session, describe in your own words how law-keeping has been dramatically altered under the terms of the new covenant?

11.     Does God have a different expectation for our behavior now under the terms of the new covenant? Discuss the rationale for your answer based upon Scripture.

Whereas under the old covenant men had to keep the Torah out from the energy of their flesh, under the new covenant we are enabled to behave righteously out from the energy of the indwelling Holy Spirit.

> *The kind of faith that saves is demonstrated by a lifestyle that is righteous and holy.*

12.     In your opinion, what aspects, if any, of the Torah no longer apply under the new covenant? Discuss the rationale for your answer based upon Scripture.

The Law of Moses given in the Torah is complex, weaving various types of law in its narrative. You might ask the question, "does the entire law as written apply today?" Are there portions of the law that have found their complete fulfillment in Christ and are therefore inoperative today? Think of the Mosaic law in these terms:

- **The moral law**, consisting of the Ten Commandments of Exodus 20:1-17, which are repeated in Deuteronomy 5:5-21.

- **The civil or case law** which appears throughout the books of Exodus, Leviticus and Numbers, and is repeated in condensed form in Deuteronomy. Civil or case law sets forth the practical implications of the moral law for specific situations as a means for governing society.

- **The religious or ceremonial law** is primarily found in Leviticus, but also appears in Exodus and Numbers; a condensed version of it is included in Deuteronomy. This component of the law sets forth the requirements for the religious life of the Israelites.

Most biblical scholars agree that only the moral law carries over to the new covenant. The civil law still stands as a divine model for ordering society, but it is not mandatory. And the religious law was instituted strictly for the nation of Israel, and it has been fulfilled through Jesus Christ's sacrifice of Himself for the sins of His people.

> *Therefore, since we have been delivered from the Mosaic law through the death of Jesus, we are not longer subject to it as an external, legalistic requirement. Instead, we desire to keep it in our hearts and lives because of the Holy Spirit's prompting and energizing.*

## The Feasts and Festivals of Israel

The feasts and festivals of Israel form a far more comprehensive and rich representation of God's redemptive program than do the events prescribed in the Christian calendar. Nevertheless, the Christian church made a decisive break with its Hebraic roots during the time of Constantine in the early 4th century AD.

13. List the major feasts and festivals prescribed in the 23rd chapter of Leviticus. Can you identify the correspondence between these feasts and festivals with the ministry of Jesus Christ?

Passover was celebrated in the early spring. It points to our salvation. Pentecost occurs 50 days later and points to our sanctification. The fall feasts of trumpets, the Day of Atonement, and Tabernacles all point to our glorification.

14.    The feasts and festivals of Yahweh afford a rich representation of our experience of redemption and salvation through the lavish grace of Yahweh. Select one of the spring feasts and one of the fall feasts and write a short paragraph explaining its representational significance.

15.    Based upon all your studies thus far, how would you represent the Torah and its relationship with your life as a disciple of Christ?

# Notes & Reflections

Use the space below to record additional insights and comments resulting from your studies thus far.

# Session 7.
# Examples from the Christian Scriptures

## The Parable of the Unforgiving Servant

**Read Matthew 18:21-35.**

1.    List the characters in this parable and who each of them represents.

2.    Describe the relationship between the amounts of money owed by the two servants; that is, the 1st servant to the king and the 2nd servant to the 1st servant.

3.    There are several lessons that can be derived from this parable. List at least three in order of importance, with the first being the most important in your view).

4.    Assuming the king in the parable represents God, and the 1st servant represents you or me, how does Jesus represent the magnitude of the sin debt that we owe to God?

5.    How does Jesus represent God's forgiveness toward us?

6.  How does the magnitude of the sin debt that we owe to one another compare to that which each of us owes to God?

7.  How does Jesus represent the ultimate moral and spiritual state of the unforgiving servant?

8.  How does He represent the consequences of an unforgiving spirit?

9.  How would you describe the connection between God's forgiveness of each of us and our forgiveness of one another?

10  Why is it that a lack of forgiveness on the part of a Christian makes absolutely no sense in the light of this biblical representation?

11. What is a biblical representation of other people's offenses against us as compared with our intuition-based representation?

As we have seen, this rich parable is replete with important representations regarding sin and forgiveness. The king represents God the Father, and the servants represent people like you and me. The amount of money owed by the 1st servant to the king was so huge that it would have required multiple lifetimes for him to repay it. But the amount of money owed by the 2nd servant to the 1st was equivalent to several months' worth of a day laborer's wages.

In the parable, Jesus teaches us how we should represent sin in general; that is, sin is an offense which creates a moral liability or debt, like the monetary debt we might owe a bank. In particular, He teaches us how we should represent the sin debt which each of us owes to God on account of the offenses we have committed against Him. And Jesus teaches us how we should represent the sin debt that we owe one another on account of the offenses we commit against one another.

In the financial crisis of 2008, many people in the United States suddenly discovered that their mortgage debts far exceeded the value of their homes. Moreover, multitudes were laid off from their jobs, meaning that they lost the ability to make mortgage payments. Imagine yourself being in this situation. How surprised and delighted you would be if the bank were to forgive your entire mortgage debt rather than foreclosing on your mortgage. Such was the situation of the 1st servant in the parable.

We identified several important representations from this parable as follows:

- **Sin**. All human sin creates a moral debt owed by the offender to the one offended.

- **God's forgiveness**. The moral debt that we owe to God is astronomical in comparison to any debt another person might owe to us. Because God forgave our enormous debt, we, in response, should freely forgive one another.

- **Our forgiveness of others**. The essence of forgiveness is an act of the will whereby the offended party wipes the slate clean of the moral debt owed to him by the offender. Although in the parable both parties begged for forgiveness, forgiveness need not be dependent on an apology from the offender.

- **Moral state of the unforgiving person**. An unforgiving spirit may indicate we have never really trusted Christ and internalized God's forgiveness of us.

- **God's forgiveness should motivate our forgiveness**. God has graciously forgiven the enormous debt which each of us owed to Him on account of our sin. If we truly internalize this fact, then it should constrain and compel us to forgive those who have offended us, no matter how great or small the offense. In so doing, we are demonstrating our heartfelt gratitude for the grace of God toward us, and we are reflecting that grace toward others.

12. Examine your own life. What action should you take if you can identify a person who may have offended you?


# The Prodigal Son – Restored Relationship

**Read Luke 15:1-32.**

By carefully reading the entire chapter, you should be able to discover clues as to the thrust of Jesus' teaching in the parables of the Lost Sheep, the Lost Coin, and the Prodigal Son.

13. What clues did you discover? What would you say is the overall thrust of the chapter? What contribution do each of the three parables make to the overall thrust?

14.   List the characters in the Prodigal Son parable together with a brief summary of their actions.

15.   What heart attitude does the younger son display toward his father?

## Read Deuteronomy 21:18-21.

16.   Based upon this passage in the 21$^{st}$ chapter of Deuteronomy, how would you represent God's assessment of the younger son's attitude and resulting behavior?

17.   As the parable unfolds, what representation of his inheritance does the younger son's behavior reveal?

18.   As the son reflects on his condition, what course of action does he decide on?

19.   Based upon this parable, how would you represent the act of repentance?

Repentance is not merely feeling sorry for our sin; it is a profound recognition of the extent of our sin, hating it, and turning from it.

20.   How does Jesus represent the relationship between repentance and saving faith through the younger son's words when he returned to his father?

21.   How would you represent the father's response to the return of his wayward younger son?

22.   How would you represent the older son's response to his brother's return and the lavishly gracious manner in which his father had welcomed him home?

23.   Is Jesus placing in evidence a serious moral issue through the words and actions of the older son?   If so, how would you represent this moral issue?

**Read Luke 18:9-14.**

24.   How would you represent the two people in this parable?  Do you see any parallels or correspondences between these two people and the two sons in the Prodigal Son parable?

25.      What other parables and teachings of Jesus address the two kinds of people you identified in the answer to the previous question? Can you identify any passages in the Hebrew Scriptures which teach the same principle? Would you say this is a recurring biblical theme? What is the significance of the repetition of this theme?

26.      How did the older son represent his own moral state in comparison with that of his younger brother? How would Jesus represent the moral state of the two brothers as the parable comes to its conclusion?

27.      Reflecting on the entire trajectory of this parable, at what points in the younger son's experience do you perceive God's blessing and God's cursing? What was the factor which triggered the blessing and the cursing?

The parable of the prodigal son is a timeless story of unconditional forgiveness. In the culture of that day, it was unthinkable for a son to ask for his inheritance while his father was still living. Family and land were God's promise to Abraham, and were highly valued by the Israelites. Therefore, the younger son showed his father great disrespect with his request. It was as if he wanted his father to die prematurely! Yet, in spite of this, the father met his son's request by selling a portion of his land and livestock and giving him the proceeds of the sale.

You know the story. This son then moves to a foreign country where he squanders his money and is forced to sell himself into slavery as an indentured servant feeding pigs – a totally despicable occupation for a Jewish man. Coming to the end of himself, he casts himself on the mercy of his father. He approaches his father with a truly penitent heart, begging his forgiveness. This is what saving faith looks like: profound trust in and casting oneself upon the mercy and forgiveness of God.

The wayward son deserved to be stoned to death in accordance with the passage in the 21$^{st}$ chapter of Deuteronomy. However, instead the fatted calf was prepared. Even as the father lavishly celebrated the return of his wayward son, there is rejoicing in heaven when a single person repents of his prideful rebellion against God, receives the forgiveness which Jesus procured for him at such a horrendous cost, and becomes a fully devoted follower of Jesus Christ.

Now let's reflect on the attitude of the older son as revealed through his words and behavior. Humanly speaking, we might say that the older son had the right to be jealous of his younger brother, especially in the light of his father's expansive reception of him. However, in the light of our study on forgiveness, we see that the father exhibited the godly response, whereas the older son's response was ungodly. The older son considered himself as morally superior to his younger brother, and he refused to embrace his father's lavish grace toward him.

To be in fellowship with God the Father, is true blessing; to be removed from that fellowship is the essence of cursing. In fact, the very essence of salvation from evil, sin, and death is to be restored to fellowship with the living God. Another principle we derive from this parable is that God delights in those who wholeheartedly repent of their sin and cast themselves upon His mercy. However, He detests those who are pridefully self-righteous, and who represent themselves as not needing to repent.

28.　　Examine your own life. What attitude toward sin is manifested by your words and actions: the contrition and repentance of the younger son or the prideful self-righteousness of the older son?

## Other Examples from the Christian Scriptures

The Christian Scriptures are replete with representational teaching. In fact, in Session 1 we touched on several examples to impart an understanding of the idea of biblical representations. Now, as I draw Session 7 to its conclusion, I will direct your attention to several more.

**Read Ephesians 1:3-14.**

29.     According to this passage, how does God the Father represent you as a disciple of Jesus Christ? On what basis does this representation apply?

**Read Deuteronomy 8:1-20, Luke 12:13-21, Luke 14:25-33, 2 Corinthians 9:1-5, Philippians 3:7-11, and 1 Timothy 6:3-10.**

30.     How should the disciple of Christ represent material wealth, prosperity, and comfort in relation to knowing Christ and being a citizen of God's kingdom? What is the ultimate source of material wealth? What are the implications of this fact?

**Read Isaiah 57:15, Isaiah 66:2, Luke 14:7-11, Romans 12:16, Philippians 2:1-11, James 4:6-10, and 1 Peter 5:5-7.**

31.     According to these passages, how should the disciple of Christ represent himself in relation to God and other people?

**Read Acts 16:16-34, Romans 5:1-5, Hebrews 12:1-14, James 1:2-4, and 1 Peter 3:13-18.**

32.     According to these passages, how should the disciple of Christ represent physical afflictions, tribulations, and sufferings?

**Read 2 Corinthians 4:16-5:5 and Philippians 1:12-30.**

33.     How should a disciple of Christ represent decline of physical powers with age, leading ultimately to physical death?

# Notes & Reflections

Use the space below to record additional insights and comments resulting from your studies thus far.

# Session 8.
# Building a Biblical Worldview

James, the half brother of Jesus, gives us seven pointers in the 1st chapter of his short epistle that direct us to embrace and build a biblical representational world, by means of which we perceive people, events, circumstances, and things in accordance with the power, love and promises of God, and NOT in accordance with our own natural intuition, lived experiences, or human wisdom apart from God.

> **James 1:2-4.** Consider it a great joy, my brothers, whenever you experience various trials, knowing that the testing of your faith produces endurance. But endurance must do its complete work, so that you may be mature and complete, lacking nothing.

1. In accordance with natural intuition, lived experiences, and human wisdom apart from God, how do we represent trials, testings, and afflictions? What is the biblical representation of these things?

> **James 1:5-8.** Now if any of you lacks wisdom, he should ask God, who gives to all generously and without criticizing, and it will be given to him. But let him ask in faith without doubting. For the doubter is like the surging sea, driven and tossed by the wind. That person should not expect to receive anything from the Lord. An indecisive man is unstable in all his ways.

2. Given the context, why is it that we should ask God for wisdom?

**James 1:9-11.** The brother of humble circumstances should boast in his exaltation, but the one who is rich should boast in his humiliation because he will pass away like a flower of the field. For the sun rises with its scorching heat and dries up the grass; its flower falls off, and its beautiful appearance is destroyed. In the same way, the rich man will wither away while pursuing his activities.

3.    What is the representational issue addressed in this passage?

**James 1:12.** A man who endures trials is blessed, because when he passes the test he will receive the crown of life that God has promised to those who love Him.

4.    Why is it so important for us to persevere in the face of trials?

**James 1:13-16.** No one undergoing a trial should say, "I am being tempted by God." For God is not tempted by evil, and He Himself doesn't tempt anyone. But each person is tempted when he is drawn away and enticed by his own evil desires. Then after desire has conceived, it gives birth to sin, and when sin is fully grown, it gives birth to death.

5.    What representational issue is addressed by this passage? Is there a difference between a trial and a temptation? Explain the rationale for your answer.

**James 1:17.** Don't be deceived, my dearly loved brothers. Every generous act and every perfect gift is from above, coming down from the Father of lights; with Him there is no variation or shadow cast by turning.

6. What representational issue is addressed by this passage? Why is it important?

**James 1:18.** By His own choice, He gave us a new birth by the message of truth so that we would be the firstfruits of His creatures.

**Also read Exodus 23:16-19, Exodus 34:22-26, Leviticus 2:12-2:14, and Leviticus 23:10-20.**

In James 1:8 the Apostle represents us as "the firstfruits of His creatures". The law of the firstfruits offering is set forth in the passages from Exodus and Leviticus.

7. With the law of the firstfruits offering as background, what is the representational significance of James' referring to us as the firstfruits of God's creatures in James 1:8?

The epistle of James contains very practical "rubber meets the road" teaching, which is sharply focused upon our living out what we believe. James' teaching guides us in the task of governing our thoughts, words, and actions in accordance with biblical reality. The following list summarizes the seven representational issues addressed in the 1st chapter of James:

■ God uses trials to move us along the path toward spiritual maturity – that is, conformity to image of Christ.

■ Wisdom is available for the asking; it is especially needed in the context of trials so we can respond to them in a godly way.

■ God views those of lowly circumstances as exalted, and the rich as abased.

■ We need to exercise patient endurance under trial in order to receive the crown of life.

■ Temptations are solicitations to evil, and they originate in our own fallen natures.

■ God is the giver of good gifts.

■ God blesses His children with material wealth in order that we, in turn, can be a blessing to others.

Building a biblical worldview does not come through osmosis. It requires work on our part. A biblical worldview is dependent upon our knowing and applying the principles of Scripture; it is the product of diligent study and lifelong practice.

It also requires conscious rejection of the world's view of reality. The media would have us believe that life is "all about us". But God says we are to deny ourselves. A biblical worldview is both counter-intuitive and counter-cultural. It takes a great deal of courage and self-control to go against the flow. However, the eternal reward far outweighs whatever sacrifice or affliction we are called upon to endure in this life.

Allow me to conclude this session by quoting once again Yahweh's instruction to Joshua:

> **Joshua 1:8-9.** This book of instruction must not depart from your mouth; you are to recite it day and night so that you may carefully observe everything written in it. For then you will prosper and succeed in whatever you do. Haven't I commanded you: be strong and courageous? Do not be

afraid or discouraged, for Yahweh your Elohim is with you wherever you go.  [Adapted from the HCSB]

## Notes & Reflections

Use the space below to record additional insights and commentary resulting from your studies thus far.

# Session 9.
# Review & Discussion

In this study we have learned that perceiving persons, events, circumstances, and things in accordance with a godly representational world (see Figure 1 and associated discussion) is life-critical. Living as a true disciple of Christ is impossible unless we learn and diligently practice this principle.

Life is often difficult. Natural and human-caused tragedies abound. Satan, the enemy of our souls, is constantly at work, and he seeks to defeat us at every turn. Even as was the case with our first parents in the Garden, his attacks are always based upon misrepresentations. Which means that our counterattacks must be based up true, biblical representations. Regarding Satan himself, the foremost of these is that Jesus Christ vanquished him through His death. Thus, we can always resist him in the name of Jesus Christ.

When tragedy strikes, victory is achieved by representing God in accordance with the faith of Jesus Christ (see Figure 3 and the associated discussion in Session 2). The first component of the faith of Jesus Christ is that the Father's love for His children – those who are the elect and in Christ – is unshakeable. Accordingly, He allows nothing to come against or upon us that is not for our good and His glory. Review the concepts that we discussed in Sessions 1 and 2 until you have internalized them.

Our faith is most sorely tested when adversity confronts us. In the face of adversity, we must learn to practice the following Scripture:

> **Ephesians 3:10-11.** This is so God's multi-faceted wisdom may now be made known through the church to the rulers and authorities in the heavens. This is according to His eternal purpose accomplished in the Messiah, Jesus our Lord.

The great biblical example of this Scripture in operation is found in the story of Job. By God's own testimony, Job "was a man of perfect integrity, who feared God and turned away from evil." The severe trials that God allowed Satan to unleash against Job placed in evidence the manifold wisdom of God before Satan and his demons.  In particular, that manifold wisdom was manifested by Job's maintaining his integrity in the face of Satan's fierce attacks.

In the 19th chapter of the book which bears his name, we find the following ringing testimony of Job's faith in resurrection:

### Job 19:23-27.

> I wish that my words were written down,
>> that they were recorded on a scroll
>> or were inscribed in stone forever
>>> by an iron stylus and lead!
> But I know my living Redeemer,
>> and He will stand on the dust at last.
> Even after my skin has been destroyed,
>> yet I will see God in my flesh.
> I will see Him myself;
>> my eyes will look at Him, and not as a stranger.

Note that this testimony from the lips of Job demonstrates that the faith of Jesus Christ was living in him.  And it enabled him to view reality according to the mind of Christ.

And so God's purpose in allowing trials, testings, and afflictions to come against us can be summarized by the following three points.

- To strengthen, establish, and mature us in our faith – that is, to cause the faith of Jesus Christ to be the dominant force in our lives, enabling us to perceive all persons, events, circumstances, and things in accordance with the mind of Christ.

- To demonstrate the manifold wisdom of God to "the rulers and authorities in the heavens" in accordance with Ephesians 3:10-11 and as exemplified by the story of Job.

- To demonstrate the manifold wisdom of God to the natural world.

Our challenge, then, is to fill our minds with Scripture, to reflect on it and absorb its principles into the warp and woof of our very souls in accordance with Joshua 1:8. As we do this, we allow the Holy Spirit of God to guide and direct our thought process so we come to have and be governed by the mind of Christ. As we view the world in accordance with the faith of Jesus Christ, we will see with increasing clarity the working of God in the midst of trials, testings, afflictions, and even tragedies.

Charles Stanley once said, "Remember, you first win spiritual victories in your mind. If you cave in to feelings of fear and doubt, you will lose."

The choice is ours. We can walk in the flesh, or we can walk in the spirit. We can walk in the way of the world, or we can walk in the way of Christ. We can walk in the way of fear, or we can walk in the way of faith.

Faith or fear; which will you choose?

# Discussion Questions

1. Discuss the concepts of the godly and ungodly representational worlds in relation to your own thought process. Which one comes naturally, and which requires mental effort?

2. Why is it important to discard the ungodly representation world? Can this be accomplished all at once, or does it require a lifetime of discipline and practice?

3. Select two biblical representations other than those discussed in this study guide, one from the Hebrew Scriptures and the other from the Christian Scriptures. Analyze and discuss the significance of each. Is the representation normative? What

practical lessons do you derive from the two biblical representations?

4.     Our representational world impacts our emotions, will, and behavior. Identify and discuss a specific area of your life and ministry in which you have practiced an ungodly representational world. What was the outcome? What difference would it have made if you had operated with a godly representational world?

5.     How have you been impacted by the insights gained from this study guide? Discuss ways in which the thrust of your life will be altered by putting those insights into practice.

6.     We have linked our natural intuition and lived experiences apart from God with an ungodly representational world. What happens to our intuition as a result of the sanctification process as we become more and more conformed to the image of Christ? What happens to our intuition as we learn to consistently practice a godly representational world?

7.     In what ways will the insights gained from this study impact your approach to sharing your faith with family members, friends, neighbors, classmates, and work associates?

8.     Share with your study group a personal example of viewing a difficult situation in your life from God's perspective. How was your faith challenged and what was the result?

9.     By applying what you have learned in this study of biblical reality, analyze the representational content of the components of the Christian's defensive armor and offensive weaponry as set forth by the Apostle Paul in Ephesians 6:10-20. (**Hint**: Pay special attention to the shield of faith.)

10.    What are some practical steps you can take to develop and strengthen your own godly representational world toward the goal of having and being governed by the mind of Christ in every arena of life, including family, church, employment, and politics?

## Notes & Reflections

Use the space below to record additional insights and comments resulting from your studies thus far.

# Walking in the Way of Christ & the Apostles

## Study Guide Series (SGs)

**Part 1 – Foundational Concepts**. These concepts are foundational to equip the Christ-follower to have and to be governed by the mind of Christ.

     1.     The Way of God
     2.     The Storyline of the Bible
     3.     Biblical Reality
     4.     Discovering the Meaning of Scripture
     5.     Torah: The Fountainhead of Wisdom
     6.     The Two-Part Christian Gospel

**Part 2 – The Gospel of the Kingdom of God**. Here we explore the ways in which the Christian gospel confronts the prideful rebellion of the human heart and exalts Christ as King over all.

     7.     Authority of the King
     8.     Called by the King
     9.     Meaning of Discipleship
     10.     Disciplines of the Kingdom
     11.     Household of the King
     12.     Second Coming of the King

**Part 3 – The Gospel of God**. This final set explores how the Christian gospel affords a complete solution to human depravity and the threefold problem of evil, sin, and death.

     13.     Introduction to the Gospel of God
     14.     Reason for the Gospel of God
     15.     Content of the Gospel of God
     16.     Perversions of the Gospel of God
     17.     Application of the Gospel of God

## Theological Readers (TRs)

TR1 – Part 1: Foundational Concepts
TR2 – Part 2: The Gospel of the Kingdom of God
TR3 – Part 3: The Gospel of God
TR4 – Resources and Appendices

Connect with us at www.DaystarInstituteNM.us, or
Contact us via email at WalkingintheWayUSA@gmail.com

WitW
Walking in the Way of
Christ & the Apostles

www.ingramcontent.com/pod-product-compliance
Lightning Source LLC
Chambersburg PA
CBHW071926020426
42331CB00010B/2737